COMES JUDGMENT

Tom Hoskins

Fulton Books, Inc.
Meadville, PA

Published by Fulton Books 2020

ISBN 978-1-64952-366-2 (paperback)
ISBN 978-1-64952-367-9 (digital)

Printed in the United States of America

CONTENTS

ACKNOWLEDGMENTS

The author wishes to thank you, the reader, for stopping long enough to flip through this book. It is only by venturing into new territory that we grow. I hope you find the contents enticing and useful. Each of us needs to grow intellectually and emotionally until our time is up. Hopefully, that will be many productive and fulfilling years from now.

The author also wants to thank and recognize his parents, brothers and sisters, and all his other relatives. In addition, this book is dedicated to every person he has ever met. Those who have encouraged and supported are to be commended. In addition, those who have opposed or challenged have helped round out the thinking process and belief system promoted by this body of information. Even those who smile and say hello, or frown and ignore make an impact on others. Hopefully, the reader will offer the former to those he encounters.

As a teacher, I benefited from so many wonderful educators as well as every student that walked through my door. In these troubled and confusing times, I pray that teaching and learning will continue in factual and helpful ways across the board. I have had many dear friends that have helped shape my thinking and will forever appreciate their company. In particular, I want to thank Suzanne and Karlee at Fulton books for their support and assistance with the publishing process.

My most sincere thanks are reserved for my children, Brian and Jennifer, and for helping me develop throughout our years together. They are most precious. My dear wife, Dorothy, has influenced and molded me in more ways than anyone. Thank you. The most profound influence and changes must be given to the one who brought all these into focus, Jesus Christ, my Lord and Savior. May he bless you as well.

Thank you.

INTRODUCTION

These are times that try men's souls. Okay, so I borrowed that from Thomas Paine. As I pen these words (rather tap them) the television in the other room is blaring about impeaching Donald Trump and wondering if the assassination of an Iranian leader might ignite a war between Iran and the United States of America. Tom was right! How many fears and worries were just triggered?

Interestingly, one must believe in the soul if it is to be tried. Although I am bothered by the current affairs just mentioned, my purpose in writing this book is to ponder the fate of souls, which I definitely do believe in. Actually, it is a matter of life and death...eternal life and death. Hebrews 9:27 says, "And as it is appointed unto men once to die, but after this the judgment." Meaning mankind, of course. We ponder our existence from time to time, especially in times like these. Perhaps you would like to explore the possibilities with me? I hope so. It's your call and your money. Please consider this book. It is not written for Bible scholars, but for the rest of us.

The reader will notice quite early on that I have appropriated most of the words and ideas that you will read. It recently occurred to me that almost every thought we have is not really ours alone. We reflect the totality of experiences we have gone through. I still say things I learned from my dad that get me in trouble. I'm sure you understand. My hope is to share what I have learned from my Lord about life on earth and life after our life is done on earth. I do so enjoy simplicity, so I will often use expressions and quotes like Mr. Paine's above. They are most often simple but can also be quite profound at the same time. My hope is they will make the reader feel comfortable, like an old friend, and at the same time convey the point being made. It would be nice if they were also accurate and true. The author will do his best to ensure accuracy. Honest to God!

Some will rejoice at the subject of judgment, and some will be put off. Know that I care about both. I am not here to judge, but to discuss judgment. Once the concept popped into my brain, I have felt compelled to share the topic. If I did nothing about it, I would feel unhappy with myself. I do feel led, so I will lean not only on my friends, my experiences, the expressions and quotes I use, but also the Word of God. Both the reader and my Lord will judge whether I did the subject justice. Whether well or poorly done, I will be satisfied because I tried. "For I am not ashamed of the gospel of Christ for it is the power of God unto salvation" (Romans 1:16).

Thank you.

COMES JUDGMENT

"And it is appointed unto men once to die, but after this the judgment" (Hebrews 9:27). There does not seem to be any room for challenge here. One might not understand the quote or might not believe it, but the statement in Hebrews still stands. One may challenge judgment, ignore it, or think it unfair. The statement remains. I do not make the statement. It comes from the Word of God mentioned above. Nor do I judge anyone. I lack the authority. Nevertheless, I feel compelled to warn those who are unaware. I would hope anyone who understands the words would be concerned enough for those around him to point it out as well. The statement is a warning to all mankind, not just those born of the male gender. Ignore it at your own personal risk!

I intend to explore the idea of judgment for the remainder of this book. I am well aware judgment is not a new concept, nor is it particularly welcomed by all. Judgment remains. We cannot wish it away. Denying it does not prevent it. If you are summoned to appear before a judge, I do not advise ignoring the subpoena or challenging it. A wise person would want to avoid nasty consequences. You may appear in court to challenge the case before the court but be advised that you are NOT the judge. If you forget, you will be reminded. Good luck!

As a young boy, I was aware of doing things not permitted and found myself being judged. Very unpleasant circumstances we all have experienced. Judgment is. People are more than willing to point out our mistakes. On the other hand, we have all experienced positive judgment as well. Those were all welcome and pleasing. We love to hear "Bravo, way to go!" I especially look forward to hearing "Well done, thou good and faithful servant" (Matthew 25:21). The strange thing is that most of us even judge ourselves. Hopefully, this leads to our improvement over time. I always tried to be lenient on myself though. Without these evaluations of our actions, we would almost certainly find ourselves in all kinds of trouble. I am thankful these "court appearances" have kept me on track for so many years. Society would certainly be chaotic if rules did not exist and acceptable conduct were not judged.

It would seem rather obvious that the judgment being explored here is of a more serious nature. More precise, life and death. Even more precise, eternal life and death. Judgment remains. With or without our approval, there is judgment and there is a judge, namely, God. One may not like it, but I am glad God has the authority since he knows how to enforce it with love and care. I am grateful I do not have the burden and I would be afraid of my own judgment. I do not know anyone on earth I would place my eternal life with. There are untold numbers of people out there who believe they can judge themselves. Some try offering that there is no judgment. That is an error in judgment.

"For God shall bring every work into judgment" (Ecclesiastes 12:14). No ifs, ands, or buts about it! It does not say God might. "And they were judged, every man, according to their works" (Revelation 20:13). "For the Father judgeth no man, but hath committed all judgment unto the Son" (John 5:22). The very next verse states, "Anyone who believes in Christ shall have eternal life and shall not come into judgment but is passed from death unto life."

Wow! Clear as a bell. There are so many statements supporting this claim that I would be hard-pressed to number them all. The reader might choose to reject these claims but would have to deny the Bible and Christ himself to do so. Permit me to make the case for the veracity of both if you would be so kind.

Permit me a quick aside as well. Some would think me arrogant or self-righteous for trying to cram this down their throat. They may do so, but I plead innocence. I do not make the claims about judgment but am merely a messenger. Neither do I pass judgment on anyone, since the Bible makes it crystal clear that we are to "judge not, that ye be not judged" (Matt. 7:1). It does, however, encourage me to share the Gospel with as many as I possibly can.

As for the veracity of the Bible, I will have to get in line behind hundreds of Bible scholars. Since I do not wish to burden you with that much homework, let me refer you to two that are both excellent and written for the layman.

Evidence That Demands a Verdict by Josh McDowell got me started and excited many years ago and *The Case for Christ* by Lee Strobel more recently. Life-changing! Having satisfied my desire to know the truth about the accuracy of the Bible years ago, I have been blessed to then discover its wisdom and truth and incorporate it into my life. Since some of the readers of this book have not had the opportunity or enough time to investigate the "good book," allow me to present a few helpful facts that might put their minds at rest. A doubtful mind can be a real stumbling block.

They say seeing is believing, but modern photoshopping and altering images on your phone can make you either beautiful or ugly. What is this world coming to? One must be careful to verify things today. I never saw Jesus, Mary, Paul, or John the Apostle, so how am I to believe in them? The answer lies in witnesses and truthful accounts. I never saw Abraham Lincoln or George Washington either, but I believe they were amazing presidents who touched many lives. The witnesses involved in their lives have passed on the stories about their lives. I have doubts about the cherry tree and am sure Lincoln didn't sleep in every home that people say he did, but the tales and the truth are pretty clear. The people who witnessed Jesus and the others might have been ill-educated, but they knew what they saw and heard. Eyewitnesses.

As to the Bible being an accurate record, there are many opinions, but the accounts were put down in writing at a time when hundreds of witnesses could verify the truth or falsehood of the record. Matthew was written only twenty years after Jesus was crucified. If he wrote down things that were untrue, hundreds of people would have set the record straight. According to Paul in 1 Corinthians 15:6, more than five hundred people saw Jesus after he was crucified and buried in Jerusalem. If it did not happen, there were people alive when the book was written who could have objected. Likewise, Mark was written about thirty-eight years after Christ; Luke, about thirty years after Christ; and John, about fifty years after he walked with Jesus. Seeing is believing! Many of those witnesses became martyrs because they would not deny what they saw. Very convincing to me. You can believe them or not. That is the most precious thing we enjoy here in the US of A, freedom to choose.

In addition to the events and witnesses described above, let me tell about the rest of the story. Scoffers will be quick to point out that the events and witnesses I used were taken from the Gospels and other Bible sources, so they are fake news from old times. Something meeting the needs of this author. Fair claims, except that desiring to know the whole truth and nothing but the truth, other witnesses have penned the events described. Others, mind you, who were anything but Christians. Witnesses who had no dog in the hunt. The most well-known is a man known as Josephus. A man who recorded events on behalf of Rome itself. He was paid by the Romans to keep watch on those pesky Jews. He was born in Jerusalem in AD 37 and recorded the events of the day.

This historian wrote a book called *Antiquities of the Jews*. In the book, he describes how Pontius Pilate—the governor of Judea, under the rule of Tiberius, the second Roman emperor—had Jesus, the brother of James, crucified. An outside account of the characters and events. Mind you, Josephus viewed it all from a different perspective than the Bible. Nevertheless, he recorded that "Jesus, the man, if it be accurate to call him a man," was seen by many who claimed to see him walking around three days later. Resurrected! He also referred to John the Baptist. He could not have obtained the facts from the Bible, since it was not even circulated yet. Another Roman historian named Tacitus recorded the same crucifixion in a book written around AD 115 to 117. I am so grateful that information is recorded so that history can be viewed in the hope we can all benefit from it.

People in the Bible, I believe, were not Walt Disney characters. Herod was real, the Pharisees were real, Caiaphas was the high priest at the time. Even Barabbas, the zealot murderer, was recorded in books outside the Bible. He was imprisoned for murdering Roman soldiers. The events described during that particular time when Jews were celebrating the Passover have changed our world forever. Those who choose to believe it never happened are confronting recorded facts that even nonbelievers wrote down. I encourage the reader to ponder the record of the events and search the records to find any significance for his own life. In addition, he should be aware that facts alone will not resolve the question. It is a matter of the heart as well.

The matter of Jesus's resurrection is profoundly significant as well. Let's consider it. There is probably no other event that has happened in history that has had such dramatic effects on people's lives and historical events. There have been religious wars, profound changes in lives and national histories dictated upon the truth or falsehood of the resurrection of Jesus Christ. There were hundreds of people who were put to death because they "bet their life" on it. As mentioned above, the Bible is only one record of the martyrs for Christ. Roman history recorded the gruesome carnage in their still-famous coliseums. Not just made for movie fodder for Cecil B. DeMille.

The Bible records the events through several people in many different ways, since each of us sees things from our own perspective. Witnesses rarely explain their experiences exactly the same. I believe that lends to credibility rather than detracting from it. Luke begins the narrative with the actions of a certain man named Joseph of Arimathea. It seems he was moved to provide his own tomb, cut out of stone for the dead body of Jesus to be interred. Luke states that Joseph went to Pilate and begged for the body so Jesus could have a proper burial. Josephus also recorded this in his book mentioned above. I doubt Joseph had so much as an inkling of what was about to happen on the third day. I also believe he was much rewarded by having his own tomb available to him down the road a bit! Two for the price of one.

Luke continues his account saying two women came to the tomb on Sunday and were told by two men in shining garments that Jesus was not there but had risen as he had foretold earlier. The women even entered the empty tomb and were very afraid and upset. Mark recounts the same event but names the two women and how they were instructed to go tell Peter and the other disciples. He even describes the great stone had been rolled away and the women would not have been strong enough to move it. I surmise the women were counting on the burley guards to help them move the stone so they could deliver spices for anointing the deceased. Add this to events described above, when Jesus appeared to above five hundred people, and the evidence is more than compelling. Again, some details are provided by nonbelievers including Romans.

I'm no lawyer or forensic scientist, but I believe the testimony provided. Many people say that the events never happened, and they can make their statements until the cows come home, but I have never seen or read any convincing evidence that Jesus was not raised and missing from that tomb. I read about no thieves being caught and hanged for messing with the tomb. The disciples were not caught with the corpse. They were scared little chickens, hiding somewhere in Jerusalem. The religious Pharisees and Sadducees were enemies of Jesus the Christ and wanted him forever dead. They said he was *not* the Christ. Jesus got the last word, and so have I. Thanks for your kind attention. I want to turn mine to the rest of the story. The reader can study further if he so chooses.

JUDGMENT EXPOSED

Now that I have made my position clear and played my hand, so to speak, I wish to deal with the focus of this book. Judgment is and judgment comes. Sounds scary as hell! Heaven help us! Actually, it is, but since it is inevitable and unavoidable, perhaps we can clarify and come to grips with it in this section. Forewarned is forearmed, my friend. One need not go blindly into what awaits us as we head into the future. We cannot change what lies behind us but should be comforted that we have a great deal to say about what lies ahead. I hope the reader discovers truths that will set a bright and glorious forever after. Hope dies last, after all.

As a former science teacher, I am touched and delighted whenever I see a classroom of kids in Africa with their hands screaming *call on me, teacher, call on me. I know the answer, I studied the chapter. I want to be the best student in this class. I am determined to succeed.* Now that, my friend, is a picture of hope. I will forever remember a young lad in my seventh grade class who had such a porous social filter that when he knew the answer to a question, he could barely keep his hand up quietly for more than three to five seconds before he was wiggling in the aisle and beginning to whimper as well. The kids perfected the art of eye rolling that year. Nevertheless, they couldn't help but like Bert. He didn't mean any harm, and they recognized that. They rolled their eyes anyway.

The author has been known to desire attention just as "Bert" did. This book will be in print as soon as possible. Meanwhile, I wonder if the attention forthcoming will be something to be desired. Hope springs. I have my hand in the air, since I know the answers. There is much to be wary of though. Are slings and arrows headed my way? I doubt physical harm awaits, but *quien sabe*? I take refuge in Romans 1:16, "For I am not ashamed of the gospel of Christ: for it is the power of God unto salvation for *everyone* who believeth." I do not wish to be ashamed. Been there, done that! Perhaps my answers to the question will not be complete or fall short of their mark. Hundreds of capable scholars can provide more complete answers. Good for them. The more, the merrier.

"And as it is appointed unto men once to die, but after this the judgment" (Hebrews 9:27). That seems judgmental. Duh! It even seems unfair and unkind to most of us. Still, our acceptance or rejection of the statement from the Bible can't change reality. We may get indignant and angry, or sad and worried, but judgment remains according to scripture. Refer to the last chapter to establish your own position on scripture. In the author's study is a card saying, "*Vocatus et non vocatus, Deus adem.*" Greek for "Bidden or not bidden, God remains." Wow! You mean it doesn't matter what I think? Correct! Surprise, we are not in charge of the universe. Some people believe the universe is in charge of itself, but I find that hard to believe. My life makes it abundantly clear that I am not. I can call upon God the creator or not call on him. Well, at least I have a choice. It amazes me that he invites the call. The God of the universe allows us the ability to choose him or reject him. Gracious of him, I think. I don't deserve this. He knows. He extends it, anyway, thank God. I hope not to offend the reader.

As harsh as that judgment seems, it provides us with an escape clause. We can avoid having to pay for our misdeeds and unkindness. Really? As sure as you're born, the good book states, "If we confess our sins, he is faithful and just to forgive us our sins, and to cleanse us from all unrighteousness" (1 John 1:9). What? No judgment to hell? Eternal life in heaven? Yup. Sounds like a no brainer to me. And yet there is a problem. Many people either do not believe the offer, or do not believe they should be judged by anyone. Sorry, but *Deus adem*. Truth be known, many of us would not want to forgive even ourselves. If we ask forgiveness of the Lord, he will freely give it. What an incredible offer. God's gift to man! Be advised, you cannot unwrap a gift you do not accept. Oh, what a glorious gift. It may sound positively ridiculous, but don't look a gift horse in the mouth. I wonder how that came into being? Again, your call.

A friend of mine believes that there are only two who can forgive. The one who committed the wrong (sin) and the one who was sinned against. If that is true, we are all damned because we have all wronged someone who will *never* forgive us. The good Lord knew better than to leave judgment and forgiveness in our hands. Please do not misconstrue this to mean we should not be forgiving, because we should. However, eternal forgiveness is not really in our power. Nevertheless, a forgiving person is wonderful to be around. In John 3:16, it says, not only that those who believe in Jesus are forgiven, but that they shall have eternal life and avoid judgment for the wrongs they have committed.

To many people, judgment is a negative word. You often hear, "Who are you to judge?" More than likely, the person they are talking to has some things to answer for themselves. I contend that everyone in existence has some things to answer for. To be held accountable. Still, is judgment a bad thing?

We interrupt this book to bring you an important message from the President of the United States... The coronavirus is coming to get us! What? A virus that began infecting people in Wuhan province in China has infected 75,000 people in Italy and about 7,500 of them have died. About 20 percent of those infected are medical personnel. It has now spread to the United States and all around the world, making it a pandemic. There have been other pandemics, but nothing quite like this. Here in California we are told not to go out and contact anyone without special social distancing precautions. Taking my daily run, I saw all the restaurants closed, all bars closed, most hotels, and churches are not meeting on Sunday. I usually see two or three contrails in the sky at a time. During my forty-five-minute run, I saw zero. No planes headed north or south. Uh oh! What now?

New York, Washington state, and California on a type of home lockdown to avoid something we can't even see. Little things mean a lot! The virus has the whole world wondering what is next.

Grandparents are not visiting grandkids, people are not shaking hands hello. Are we all gonna die? Of course not, but thousands already have, and many more will. The vast majority of those infected will survive and thrive. Those in their sixties to eighties are in a serious danger zone. They have a higher death rate from this than the average cold and flu virus. Many people are stressed and some panic, while hundreds frolic on the beaches in Florida. People have to stand six feet apart in lines at the grocery store, and many are standing in lines at the gun store. I guess they are going to shoot the invisible enemy. Really? Really? Every single one of them will be affected by this pandemic. Every one of them will be affected differently. How about you?

I cannot continue writing without taking a serious look at how this book about judgment matters to each of us. The unavoidable truth is we must all face death. In addition, we will all face our maker and will be offered eternal life or death. Are you ready? Are all your ducks in order? Have you taken care of business? Will there be a tomorrow for you, or is this your last day on earth? None of us knows the answer to that question, but I know that I have eternal life. The Lord has given me his promise. There is no boast in such a statement, because I am not the one who made it happen. Jesus made it possible by dying for me on a cruel cross and defeating death and coming back to life on the third day (see page 5). I am at peace. There is some sadness though. I am sad that innumerable people all over the earth do not know this peace and are not at all confident in their future or the fate of their loved ones. It need not be so.

My brother died two weeks ago. His wife told me she woke up and touched him. She shuddered to find him cold. Not even a peep! Gone forever. Our family held a memorial service and reminisced about his sixty-two years on this earth. Lots of laughter. Many tears. Everyone in the room had to realize life on earth ends. We say he is resting in peace, but God knows the truth. He knows our eternal fate after life on earth is over. God knows our eternal fate and gave us all a choice in the matter. One can ignore the choice but cannot avoid it. It is spelled out clearly in John 3:16.

Another point this writer would like to emphasize at this time: my dear brother and I had unresolved issues that kept us apart. Different opinions. Different philosophies. Our society is currently in upheaval because of the virus, but also because many are liberals and many are conservatives and cannot seem to get along. An old song asks, "When will they ever learn?" ("Blowing in the Wind"). My brother and I didn't learn in time. We can no longer bridge the gap between us. I miss you, dear Doug. Another song answers, "It's too late to say you're sorry." We cannot go back after someone is gone. Do not put off till tomorrow what needs doing today. That holds true for your choice regarding eternal life. Do not put it off.

How many times in your life have you said "I could have, I would have, I should have, *but*"? Dear reader, you need to consider this one. The choice to ask God for forgiveness for the things you have done in this life that were not good for you or someone you care about. The choice that will not only give you peace of mind but will also allow you to receive forgiveness for those things. The choice that will set you free from the burdens you have carried for far too long. Not only do you have little to lose, you have much to gain. You have everything. You have your life. Be kind to yourself this time. It's your choice!

Let us return to the place we left off. Is judgment a bad thing? If I am riding the subway home after getting off work late at night and three guys who have obviously been drinking too much get on at the next stop, I am going to judge them. If they sound happy and are enjoying each other's company, I will probably smile at them. If they say things that sound harsh and appear bothered by something, I might just wander into the next railcar. Better safe than sorry. Maybe nothing bad would have happened, but more than one passenger has avoided personal harm by being so judgmental. The Bible even tells us "to be as wise as serpents around trouble" (Mt 10:16). Sometimes it really is best to be safe than sorry. We should assume the best but be prepared for danger sometimes. Our health and safety depend upon good judgment on our part. Judgment is a blessing.

I feel blessed to live in a nation of laws in the USA. Many laws protect us from harm others might do to us and even some harm we might do to ourselves. It is good that we will have to face the judge if we go 95 mph in a 65 mph zone. We are endangering not only others, but ourselves. We appreciate accurate and precise judgment when a swimmer touches the pad 0.5 seconds ahead of the swimmer behind her. I am grateful I was also the one to judge who I wanted to spend the rest of my life with. I consider myself lucky to have made such a good choice.

The judgment we are examining here is whether we will be found not guilty or faultless for the sins (wrongs) we have committed during our entire lifetime. "All we like sheep have gone astray" (Isaiah 53:6). None of us can honestly say we are sinless. Some have done horrendous things and some relatively minor things, but everyone knows they have done things that were not right. Some get people sent to prison and some go unnoticed by any other human. Still, we know what we have done. Our Lord and Savior is aware of all and has the authority to pardon us. We have turned everyone to his own way and the Lord has laid on him the iniquity of us all. God's amazing grace says that, "If we confess our sins, he is faithful and just to forgive us our sins, and to cleanse us from all unrighteousness" (1 John 1:9). Now and forevermore. Judgment is a blessing to those who admit their sins and ask for forgiveness.

The amazing thing you will discover is that you will never be the same again. Your whole world will change for the better. You will see others in a new light. In a positive light. In a loving light. You will be pleasantly surprised to see yourself in that same light. God isn't just the judge, he is the light of this world and is love itself. He wants you to have peace and enjoy the rest of your time on earth and follow that up with eternal life in paradise. He wants you to have joy now and forever after. Yes, *I know it sounds too good to be true, but it isn't. Coming back to life after being crucified sounds too good to be true as well, but it Happened! Praise God. Praise God!*

Trust the one who overcame death and overcame the world. It might seem scary but take the leap. The leap of faith. The coronavirus can end your life on earth, but it is just a temporary thing. You will look down from heaven and shout, "Oh, death where is thy sting!" We all too often fail to realize that this world is not our home. It is a short-term experience. I'm just a poor wayfaring stranger! Some of the poets say it is but a vapor. Poof, you're gone. Please don't put it off, as many do. If you don't make a choice, you make a choice. You only have one. Trust Jesus dear one, trust Jesus.

A snail can just glide along mindlessly and a bear can crap in the woods, as they say. You, my friend, are not made the same way. They take care of physical needs and spend some time on this earth. Then it's over. Animals, weather, and bacteria do their thing. Snails and bears disintegrate and become good material for your garden. We, however, are not quite the same. Our body goes through the same biological processes, but we were created differently and for a different purpose. "Our Lord made us and formed us from the womb" (Isaiah 44:2). Additionally, Christ (our Lord on earth) made us his workmanship when we became followers (Eph. 2:10). We are here for a purpose and can make a difference. For good, or not. You are awesome, dear reader. Snails and bears are great, but *you* are awesome.

Every new day brings opportunities and choices you may or may not anticipate. Current events are even more startling. Since I passed the seventy-year mark a while back, I need to consider getting within six feet of some people. The elderly, wait, I'm elderly? We are at increased risk of death from the Coronavirus. Just close contact might be enough to infect me and subsequently, my wife. The result could be death on a ventilator without anyone besides doctors and nurses in my room. Dying does not appeal to me at this time but dying without loved ones near would be awful. I need to be careful about all my contacts. So much for saying I wouldn't touch him with a ten-foot pole. Now it makes sense.

Choices and opportunities are not limited to the physical. What we say and do has taken on new meaning these days. If we don't wear a mask or do. If we even get close in line at the grocery store, someone may become very uncomfortable or angry. Our show of respect for each other has never been more important. Many people are suffering from a variety of concerns ranging from loss of jobs, being out of school, being insecure and scared to even losing a friend or loved one. We each have an opportunity to be a caring positive influence to those around us.

This is not a time to be pushy, blunt, or unkind to those we encounter. I do not think telling someone they need to repent or die will be helpful. Asking how they are doing and meaning it would be the thoughtful thing to say. If the conversation turns to more serious matters, one can offer hope and encouragement about the future. If you are meeting someone you know on a personal basis, eternal events might even become approachable, but one needs to assess the person and what might be most helpful at the moment.

Did you think that you did not really matter or make a difference? Wrong! The things you do and say make a difference all the time. Think back on little things said and done to you in your life. All of them counted. Still do. The incredible thing is that you have choices as to how you react to them. Sure, people can try to control what you do. Let them try. God gave you the right to act as you choose. I pray you will choose wisely for yourself and those around you as well.

What'd I Do, Ma?

One of my greatest delights during the Christmas holy days (holidays) is to grab a bowl of popcorn and a drink, sit in my easy chair and pop my copy of "A Christmas Story" into the VCR. It stars Darren McGavin and Melinda Dillon and a delightful young boy named Ralphie, played by Peter Billingsley. Most of us think of "You'll shoot your eye out" from the movie because the story centers around his desire to receive a Red Ryder BB Gun for Christmas. There are countless memorable quotes I recall throughout the year, but one that belongs in this book is a result of Ralphie dropping the F-bomb next to his dad while changing a flat tire. When his mom is told about it, she is obligated to punish him. Demanding to know where Ralphie learned such a nasty word, he panicked and blamed his best friend, Schwartz. Sadly, Schwartz ends getting his rear end paddled and cries the famous words at the beginning of this chapter. He was totally innocent. Still, wrongs must be corrected and guilt is easily transferred to him.

Two thousand years ago, Jesus Christ was punished for wrongs he did not commit. As described earlier in this book, Christ suffered unto death at the cruel hands of Roman soldiers. I wonder if producers of the movie ever considered the comparison of the injustice done to poor Schwartz, the innocent, to the terrible injustice done to our Lord in Jerusalem so long ago. Although poor Schwartz had no idea why he was suffering, Jesus knowingly suffered to pay the penalty of sin that exists in each of us on this earth. Christ willingly gave his life so that our sins could be forgiven (1 Timothy 2:6). Many witnesses also gave their life to testify to the truth of that incredible event. I admit that I do not understand how Jesus can know all my sins. There are many books that explain how it works, but this writer accepts forgiveness based upon the events described earlier and the words of Christ himself.

Poor Schwartz may never have learned why he was punished. Many people are in the same state of confusion because they do not accept that they are sinners. They do not believe they have done anything seriously wrong. I have heard people say they have never robbed or killed anyone, have never cheated on their wife or done anything they should be punished for. Everyone knows they have done some things considered wrong, but many don't believe they should be punished. Thirty years of teaching taught me that misbehavior unpunished grows like a tumor. Some instructors, especially beginning instructors, think that students will become cooperative and work to the best of their ability if the teacher is thoughtful, competent, and easygoing. Experience taught me that they work to the best of their ability and behave when reasonable rules are clear and enforced. Absence of enforcement, punishment more often than not, leads to an unruly classroom. There should also be rewards for good conduct and effort. A well-run classroom with a good teacher, judge is wonderful to behold. Students thrive.

Ditto for our lives. If husbands, wives, children, workers, or any others who need to get things done together are allowed to do whatever they want without regard for those around them, things can get way out of whack. Marriages, jobs, and lives, in general, get destroyed without rules and guidelines to follow. Severe abuse on the job can lead to official actions against the wrongdoer. Children can be removed from abusive homes, and husbands or wives leave the relationship. Life can be unbearable for the one being wronged. Laws are put in place to prevent abuse, but often the abuse goes unreported or unpunished. Not only do the victims suffer, but those around suffer as well. Judgment is needed to protect everyone in our society. It is sad that so many injustices go unnoticed or unreported. Just as in the classroom, chaos may be the result of inaction. Chaos in the home, chaos on the job, and chaos in society.

We all belong to a world where things can be wonderful and enjoyable. We are also part of a world where quite the opposite is the norm. Laws, standards, and morals are helpful but, all too often, are not observed. Many wrongs go unpunished and cause further harm. It would be great if this were not so, but we suffer so many ills because people are given free will to make their own choices. The vast majority of people are good and caring and do their best to be considerate of others. Sadly, there are many who serve only themselves and make life hard for the rest of us. Our Creator could have made us so that nobody sinned or hurt anyone else, but we would then be designed to behave only kindly and lovingly. Because we were made to have free choice, some abuse the right. God hates sin, but allows it so that we can see what man is like and can learn that we can choose to follow his teachings if we so desire. "Surely goodness and mercy shall follow" (Psalm 23).

Although many go through life without pondering these things, God has made it quite clear that we will have to answer for the things we did, as well as some things we failed to do. Many wrongs occur because someone who could have stopped something from happening let it go or pretended not to notice. All that is necessary for evil to triumph is for good men to do nothing. It seems unkind to blame someone in such a situation, but the wrong may have been prevented. The amazing thing is that our wrongs can be forgiven by accepting Jesus Christ as our savior and receiving forgiveness for *all* the sins we ever did or will do subsequently. Amazing grace.

What then is sin? Sin is going against God's laws and directions for our life. Sometimes we purposely do things we know are not right and many times we do things wrong or sinful without even being aware we have done so. Even if we ignore or are unaware of wrongdoing, sin exists and needs to be dealt with. Sin is rebellion against God, even if we are unaware of it. He wants what is best for us, but we think we know better. We just want to do it our own way. We think we know what is best for ourselves. It doesn't matter if someone else disagrees. The boss or our parents sometimes admonish us with, "Because I said so, that's why." Look out! Someone is looking for trouble. Disobey at your own risk. Defiance of authority is not usually helpful.

God has our best interest at heart, but we, in our limited understanding may not recognize it. He alone is all knowing, but we get carried away with our own importance. A wise friend of mine told me he had a lot of problems as a result of ego. Once he understood ego got in his way, he changed his thinking and life became much richer for him. When my friend explained that EGO stood for "Ease God Out," my understanding was enriched as well. That's what friends are for. Thanks, Jim!

There are people everywhere who feel burdened by things they have done to others. Some people have even done things harmful to themselves. Forgiveness of those sins allows us to feel free from shame and guilt, which hold us back and get in our way. It is a wonderful thing to have someone forgive us for something we did wrong. It is life-changing to receive eternal forgiveness from our Lord and Savior. "Your sins are forgiven." Indescribable!

Do It Yourself

Save a few bucks, do it yourself! That has been my motto all my life. I built my own house, did the landscaping, built a beautiful pond and deck. My wife and I are quite pleased with the results of our efforts. We got what we wanted for the rest of our lives and everything came out perfect. Right! Well, we discovered a few items that could have been done just a little better, but when it was all said and done, we celebrated. Were there glitches? Of course, but look at the money we saved doing much of it by ourselves. Still, it is just stuff that could be gone with a single match or the next eight-point earthquake. We all need to keep stuff in its proper place.

This author is more concerned with the *stuff* of life that is really important and makes our world worth living in. The things that shape our life and those around us. The things that shaped our past and will shape the future ahead of us. How have we done so far? It really depends on what things one is talking about and is very dependent on our own philosophies and opinions. How do we judge the world so far? How do you judge the world so far? I believe it can make a difference to each of us. Since mankind is more responsible for our present state of affairs than any living creatures, how have we done? I'm pleased with my home and pleased with our country. So far! However, when one looks at much of human history, there is much to be desired. What stands out the most in the times that lead up to today. Let's take a quick look at our human efforts.

Our grasp of chemistry and physics is phenomenal. I taught science for thirty years and find it hard to comprehend the advances, not only in the last two hundred years, but the last twenty years. Science and technology advanced at breathtaking speed from the 1800s until the year 2000. Dynamite, big deal, we have the atom bomb. We have gone from gunpowder to nuclear warheads. Uh-oh. Oh well, mankind can handle it, right? I used to think we could use nuclear power wisely, now I just hope and pray. Don't expect this author to solve the world's energy and nuclear medicine needs. Still, mankind is impressive. Wisdom dealing with this knowledge remains to be seen. My faith in world powers and nations has taken a beating lately. Sorry.

How well have we dealt with our environment? As stated above, it depends significantly on your political, philosophical beliefs. Even twenty years back, I taught my young charges that cars, factories, and aerosols affected the atmosphere. Are we controlling the air temperatures with cars, boats, and planes? Beyond my pay grade, my friend. Nevertheless, it seems unwise to think we have no effect. Mankind needs to be held accountable. There ain't no free lunch, as they say. God and nature will let us know how we are doing. I happen to believe they are one and the same.

Neither you, dear reader, nor I can figure it all out, but we must accept that mankind, as a whole, cannot ignore the current biochemical interactions we have with our environment. Be vigilant, be involved, and know that you make a difference. Will God take care of it? Eventually, but he asked us to be good stewards in the meantime.

What have we done to each other? This is the subject I spend quite a bit of time with. What will we do with each other in the distant future? What are we going to do now? They say it ain't over till the fat lady sings. Sorry, I mean no disrespect, but the opera star is still in the wings and I hope we get it right before she takes the stage. Current affairs and events are quite alarming and should not be dealt with lightly. People seem more edgy and easily upset than just a few weeks ago. Our neighbors and the neighbors we have around the world need to understand that we really are in this together. The world today is so much smaller than it was when I was a kid.

I'm grateful America won the war with England. I'm glad that we got over it without too much pain. The devastation of most wars gives one pause though. WWI, WWII, concentration camps, Korea, Vietnam, and our current involvement in the Middle East should have taught us how harmful war is. Gee, I thought those protest songs during the sixties had all the answers. Well, one did. The answer is still "Blowin' in the Wind" (Peter, Paul, and Mary). The world leaders and generals need to put a stop to the pain and insanity. It is not too late to stop war and work together in peace. I will not hold my breath anyway. How about the religious wars? Well…

There have been many regional and national wars, but the religious wars have really put mankind in an indefensible position. The Spanish Inquisition stands out as one that demonstrates best how sinful mankind can be. Nobody really accepts that it is acceptable or justifiable to slaughter others just because they have the wrong religious beliefs. That is what happened anyway. That still happens today. Guess what, it doesn't work. The results make it clear that many innocent people die but the dominating, murdering religious groups have never overcome in the end. All that is accomplished is that too many people have died, as the song goes, and bitterness and hatred live on. Duh!

Moreover, countless people blame Christianity, Islam, or Judaism for the countless atrocities. This writer finds it confusing and maddening that nonbelievers want to place the blame on God. My Lord and Savior does not want anyone to suffer harm or unkindness. He was called the Prince of Peace for good reason. Read his history. Law-abiding and peaceful, still he was hoisted upon the cross. Among his final words were, "Father, forgive them; for they know not what they do" (Luke 23:34). Those are not the words of one who would have us kill one another over religious beliefs. Man, not God, is to be held accountable for our wars.

God should not be blamed or held responsible for what I do either. True, he gave me free will to do what I want, but he wanted me to make better choices. There are even some who avoid reaching out and trusting Jesus because of things I have said or done. I am truly sorry for these mistakes but find peace in knowing that the Lord forgives them. The human audience is a much rougher crowd! Each of us has sinned against God, but our Lord has not done these things, we have. Humankind is not very forgiving in general and needs to learn how wonderful and refreshing it is. We hang on to our grudges like a pit bull but fail to realize we are free when we let go of the judgment and move forward with our life. What a wonderful example Jesus gave us. What a wonderful example.

I know many people in my life who have suffered loss and who have been hurt by things who reject Christ because they think he should have protected them from the hurt. It really is a hard knock life. People make it thus, my friend, people cause it. Christ came to show us how to avoid the hurt and pain. He did not tell us we would lead the life of Riley. The Bible even tells us that the rain falls on the just and the unjust alike (Matthew 5:45). If Christians or any of us got a free ride, we would earn nothing. We are here to learn and grow toward love and forgiveness. We even learn from adversity caused by everyday occurrences not caused by people. I cannot totally understand someone falling to their death from an accident while on a hike. Nevertheless, Christ assures us that we are all just poor wayfaring strangers on this planet. We are bound for heaven if we accept our existence now as a preparation for something better. Rebelling and fighting God is hurtful and tragic. The forgiven are bound for glory.

TODAY IS THE DAY

Procrastinators, beware! Many things can be put off till tomorrow, but do not count on tomorrow for dealing with your eternal destination. If you don't get the car washed today, your wife may be upset but will not likely file for divorce. One never knows for sure though. If you don't make the house payment today, it might cost you a considerable sum. If one considers asking Christ for forgiveness, but orders another round instead, it could be a monumental mistake. I cannot explain why there are no do overs, but Hebrews 9:27 doesn't leave any room for doubt. You die, and you go to heaven or hell. It matters not if you approve or reject the statement. The Bible makes that irrefutable statement, and I cannot undo or ignore it. For reasons stated quite clearly early in this book, the author finds no reason to doubt the power and authority of Jesus Christ. I may have questions, but no doubts.

God has made it quite clear that he cannot abide with evil or sin. It clearly exists, but he wants nothing to do with it. Christ led a sinless life but ended up dying for our sins. It all seems impossible to us now, but Christ came to earth to give his life as a testament to God and a sacrifice and payment for the sins of all men. There are no records of Jesus breaking the 65 mph speed limit on the donkey. Nobody arrested him for stealing a candy bar from the store. No record exists of Jesus doing any wrong. A very clear record exists of his trial and execution, even though Pilate stated in the book of John that he could find no fault at all in Jesus. He sent him to the cross only because the crowd demanded it and Pilate wanted to avoid a riot in Jerusalem. There was no riot, but the world was changed forever when Christ was delivered to the soldiers who nailed Christ to the cross. It happened and was properly recorded. Changed my life!

What is amazing about his death is that he knew beforehand what was going to befall him and Christ did not make any effort to stop it. Being one with God makes it abundantly clear that he could have called down ten thousand angels to bring the process to an abrupt halt. He knowingly let it happen. He clearly states that he took on the sins of all mankind to demonstrate his power and his forgiveness and that he would be the payment for my sins and anyone else that trusted him. Christ rose from the tomb on the third day, just as he foretold, so that he could grab the attention of the world. The world was literally shaken by the event. As described earlier, history and hundreds of people witnessed the life, death, and resurrection of our Lord. To this day, there are those who say it is impossible and there are those who believe the witnesses and martyrs in Jerusalem. Those who believe and accept Christ into their life shall be forgiven and have eternal life.

If you accept that there are sins you have committed, you do not have to be burdened with them any longer. John 10:9–11 says that Christ came to give us life and save us from our sins. Christ also said, "Behold, I stand at the door, and knock" (Rev. 3:20). He will not force the door, we have to ask him to come in. It takes a tremendous leap of faith, but Christ will catch you. The problem is that we can only invite him into our life while we are living. Once we pass from this life on earth, it is too late to act. Only the living are allowed to make decisions. Kobe Bryant planned to go to a basketball game with his daughter. He knew it was foggy in LA, but he was unaware that his time was up. Thousands mourn his passing. I wonder if he made the right choice about our Lord before that helicopter crashed into the earth. His fate was sealed on that fateful day. My fate is already sealed because Christ is my heavenly pilot. Each of us is given the opportunity.

Some protest that there are some too young to understand about that choice. Others question the fate of people living in a society that does not make the salvation story available to its members. There are religions that deny salvation even exists. The definitive answers are above my pay grade. Scholars have debated the subject for ages and offer explanations, but the Bible says that God is not willing that any should suffer and provides an opportunity to each of us. I wonder about those described here but need to place the outcome in more capable hands. Nevertheless, those reading these pages are without excuse. The cat is already out of the bag.

Those who want to challenge the methods and veracity of salvation all too often try to hold back the tide. They waste precious time debating the issue only to find out that they debated it to death. Just because someone cannot understand completely how eternal life works doesn't mean it doesn't exist. We cannot argue it out of existence. One can wish it were not so but wishes do not determine our fate. Truth and knowledge determine what comes from the choices we make, and Jesus said, "I am the way, the truth, and the life." Truth is, what we think of it does not alter it in any way. Wise men seek the truth.

I wandered through my early days without giving any of this a thought. Ignorance is bliss, and I was as happy as a clam until I began teaching and until I had children of my own. Once I realized that my life could make an impact on others, especially my own dear ones, I began the search for enlightenment and understanding. Friends still want me to "lighten up," but my search led me to another world. To a world of forgiveness, grace, and joy. Sure, I have my ups and downs, but when it comes down to it, I feel secure and safe in the arms of Jesus, my Lord. As the saying goes, I am blessed.

FOR GOODNESS SAKE

We all know Santa Clause is watching, so be good for goodness sake. When I pilfered a candy bar from State Market, I was already old enough to know my Christmas gifts were not at stake. Santa was not watching me at all. My old man was a whole nother story. When I got caught, after several successful attempts, my dad made me regret I ever even liked candy. Nevertheless, most little children improve their behavior upon learning that, "Santa Claus is watching you." Parents can only get away with that threat for a limited time. I even had a pastor a few years back who got upset every year because he believed people gave Santa an ability that belongs solely to God. Pastor had a point, but I never confused Santa with God.

It is really beyond my comprehension to know the mind of God. I have enough trouble with mine! Yet the Bible states that our heavenly father knows the falling of a sparrow (Matthew 10:29), so he really must know when we have been good or bad. It also makes it abundantly clear we shall be held accountable for our deeds. To the human mind such statements make no sense. Impossible!

When I consider the cross and Christ ending his life upon it, it makes no sense either. People do not get undead. We tend to get a little too wrapped up in thinking that we can understand everything. Mankind has learned and imagined so many things over the centuries that we get carried away with ourselves. Those in Jerusalem two thousand years ago didn't have to imagine Jesus on the cross. They saw it all on CNN? Perhaps not, but there were many witnesses. Because Jesus rose to life on the third day, I feel compelled to believe he is capable of keeping a record of our existence.

How good does one have to be to go to heaven? Christ made a damning statement about you and me, along with the rest of earth's inhabitants stating, "None is good except God" (Luke 18:19). He did not mean we were worthless or good for nothing because he thought we were worth dying for. What Christ meant was that we are not pure like God. He was sinless. None of us can claim that, so we need to ask his forgiveness to be in his presence in heaven. Our Lord desires "good" company. He has prepared a divine world where goodness abounds and has planned a place for each of us in that world. Heaven knows exactly what awaits us there, but you can bet the farm it is better than anything one can purchase here on this globe.

Funerals are not the favorite event for most of us, but I am usually moved by the service, especially if the departed was someone close to me. Something quite interesting is that memorials and funerals are all similar yet each one I ever attended was distinct in some way. Often, the distinctive is a result of the life of the person being remembered. Some were well-known and some were almost unknown, but the life lived was unique. Some were really good people and a couple were rascals. Where did they go? That is the million-dollar question. Some think they remain in place, six feet below their headstone. That is a fact if only the corpse is considered, but the person's soul goes straight to heaven or hell. Do not pass go or collect $200.

The purpose of this book is to bring the reader to an understanding of the process. The "good book" tells us that to be absent from the body is to be present with the Lord if the person was a believer. The nonbeliever is destined for hell. Wow, beam me up, Scotty! Is this fair to both groups of people? As discussed above, God established both outcomes for reasons only he knows. I lament that some will not join me with our Lord in heaven but would never deign to say I know the fate of any individual. The awesome thing is that each of us has a choice in the matter. Choose wisely, dear reader. For reasons discussed earlier, the choice is inevitable regardless of what you think. I am grateful each of us has a choice.

Something that causes me a great deal of discomfort in these memorials and funerals is that so often one hears he or she was a "good person" and is resting in peace in heaven. As already mentioned, none of us is good enough, but those whose sins were forgiven are headed to a better world. Those who died in their sins are not inheriting such a wonderful existence. Is this fair? I trust our Lord alone with that determination. Again, it is above my pay grade. The thing that bothers me is that even though some mourners know the person was not a believer in Christ, they casually say the old friend went to heaven. Feels good.

Ain't true. Heaven was created not to make the world feel good but to receive those who put their trust in the one who created them and forgave them of their sins.

Although memorial services that misrepresent the salvation of the person being put to rest bother me, there are other moments related to the service that also make me uncomfortable. Some who did not even know the occupant of the hearse very well often say they will meet again with their old friend in heaven. They have no way of knowing for sure. Some of these well-meaning folks who make such statements are not even Christians themselves. They believe they have done enough good in their lives and are upward bound. If you ponder that assessment just a little, you should come to the conclusion that you have just made yourself the one who makes the final judgment. If anyone can state that they have been good enough to aspire to heaven, they have put themself in the place of the judge himself, namely, Jesus Christ. If they can make the call, the cross was an unnecessary waste of a life. God knew exactly what he was doing, and he did it for you and me. Good thing! Thank God!

RELATIVE MORALITY

I f your mind works anything like mine, you might think relative morality is what you learn from your mom and dad. The actual meaning of the term is that one's concepts of right and wrong are not the same for each of us, but can change from person to person and society to society. In other words, those things we say and do are considered right or wrong, depending upon how an individual views the actions or words. Those views would also change from place to place and society to society. The moral standards are variable. What is morally acceptable in the United States may be acceptable in the jungles of Peru. This could be cause for concern for world travelers perhaps. In reality, it is cause for concern for those who never leave their hometown because our actions can be completely acceptable to us while being offensive to a neighbor. I found this out quite early in life while eating at the home of a friend. My manners fell short of acceptable standards. What is more distressing is that I did not become aware of my somewhat crude table manners for two or three more years. My brother was kind enough to inform me two or three years later. Should have read Emily Post, I suppose.

The importance of this subject in relation to our study throughout this book is that doing good or bad can have significant consequences for our eternal salvation. We will all be judged and held accountable for our moral successes and failures. The amazing opportunity we have to avoid about judgment has been clearly pointed out in this book. This writer believes Jesus has covered our sins. The point being made here is a little different. I wish to address those who contend that this is not fair. Having dealt briefly with being judged earlier, it may help to flesh moral judgment out a bit further. In an attempt to get a clearer overall view, I spent some serious time looking into relative morality.

Wading into the large volume of literature, dealing with the subject was somewhat daunting because the subject has countless philosophers, scientists, and theologians weighing in with their opinions. After reading many pages of what relative morality is and how one should view it, I awoke to the sound of my own snoring. Thank God I didn't drool on my computer. I believe that is morally forbidden. Consequently, I am choosing to present my *Reader's Digest* version. Also, I don't think I should go on insufferably because my best friend, Larry, informed me that he resolved the issue when he was about thirteen. I believe he would explain it quite clearly.

Anyway, I reached the conclusion that God is wiser and smarter than I. The writers explaining moral relativity had a predictable problem in my humble opinion: they all disagreed with many of the beliefs of their contemporaries and those who had opined before. With so many conflicting opinions, how does one choose the correct one? Indeed, most of these wise philosophers stated that they were all correct, so there is no right or wrong. I have some serious misgivings about such confusing findings. We know on its face, there are beliefs held by many of these people that are self-serving. They would like to escape any judgment of things they have done. They clearly do not want anyone holding them accountable. Some of their behaviors are clearly unacceptable. As stated earlier, this writer feels our world would quickly become controlled by members of society who cared little for those who they wanted to take advantage of. Anarchy? Lawlessness? Most likely. I am confident it would not be pleasant for many to live in. Though we have all been judged by individuals who clearly lack credentials and have no business passing judgment, society depends on standards and rules to live by. We need to be held accountable so that society can expect reasonable standards of behavior.

Who then should be setting our standards of morality? Who is qualified? God alone meets the requirements and measures up to the standards. We are corruptible and often succumb to our own desires. We are only human, while the one who created the universe knows what is best. His desire is for the well-being of every individual. I choose to put my life in the capable hands of One who stilled the water and calmed the sea. The man from Galilee. The one who walked the earth and rose from the dead.

God has worked with mankind throughout history to instruct us on how to live a good life. There have been countless failures by individuals and whole societies, but God has provided us with a history and record to learn from. We have all too often failed to learn from the successes and failures. Humans are a stubborn lot, but Jesus came to earth to show us the way and to provide us with salvation and forgiveness. He really is the way, the truth, and the light.

Our ancient and current history make it clear that we are incapable of establishing our own morals and standards for all men and women to live by. We have a tendency to be self-serving. If morality is relative, then right and wrong can be determined by individuals and groups who may not give much thought for others. There is a moral imperative established by God. Thank God! There are some who claim there is no God and no judgment. That whatever happens, just happens. That rapists, thieves, and murderers die and end up in a grave. End of story! I am sure people like John Walsh, who had his son kidnapped, want those responsible to be held accountable. People who have had loved ones murdered want to see justice served. I believe all wrongs and human sins will come to judgment. As the saying goes, there ain't no free lunch. We must all pay unless we repent of our wrongs and allow Christ to forgive us of those sins.

0
0000

This is not my first rodeo, but I think it will be my last roundup, as depicted above. I got major eye rolls and grunts from my students over that one. I loved to make them think and used word puzzles often to reach my goal. A couple just for giggles: HELL 7 HEAVEN 5 (*Paradise Lost*). I wonder how many kids ran out and read Milton's work. Still, I always encourage them to TOTOO (put two and two together) Now you see why I had to retire.

My first rodeo as a writer is called *When I Was a Kid*. It was not my life's story. It was a plea for the reader to understand how critical, intelligent, helpful adults are to the lives of today's youth. All of us are capable of mentoring someone who needs it. Some people would do best to stay away from our young folks, while others may provide exceptional guidance and positive examples to follow. Both types exist, but my prayers are that young people would benefit from the latter. I lament that Oprah did not place the book in her book-of-the-month club. Still, hope springs eternal. I'm still available for any interview she cares to conduct. I make no apologies for the unabashed plug. I still think the book could inspire others to mentor our youth.

Sigh!

My future goals do not include another book, since I am headed for the last roundup soon enough. We all are, we just don't *know* when. Hence, the reason for this composition. I have poured out my life for those around me and can only hope the effects have been positive. Being the type of human I am, I understand that not each of these efforts got the desired results. You can lead a horse to water, but... I always tried to make sure it was potable. I also know I made some monumental blunders but take consolation in knowing that my motives were well intended. My greatest consolation is knowing that the good Lord knows all that I have done yet is gracious enough to forgive me for the failures. He lived a life demonstrating to those around him that we all need to be gracious and forgiving, but he is much better at it than us.

Although Jesus gave us a pretty good roadmap to salvation and extends his grace and forgiveness, each of us must accept that grace voluntarily, as stated numerous times throughout this book. He makes absolutely no demands upon our actions, but it is abundantly clear that he is eager to accept and forgive each of us if we ask. My desire is that you, precious reader, will see the need and wisdom to take the first step. Ask Christ into your heart, ask him for forgiveness for the things you have done wrong, even some things you did not do that you should have, and begin a new life as a blessed follower of Jesus.

Once you have taken that simple step, you may well feel compelled to share the news with those around you. Children, friends, neighbors, etc. are in need of that same forgiveness. You could be the one who brings them into a new and blessed life. One of my favorite songs is "It Only Takes a Spark (To Get a Fire Going)." That's how it is with God's love. You really matter!

A dear friend, who is not a Christian, recently stated that he believes that those who think that they know God exists and those who think that they know that God does not exist are both wrong. My friend is absolutely right. Nobody is able to answer the question regarding the existence of God irrefutably. They can only say that they believe but cannot say they know. There are always those who argue the point. The point is that *Deus adem* (God remains) whether we believe or not. For reasons proclaimed throughout this book, I believe. I also believe the alternative is not a positive way to live a life. The choice, my friend, is yours.

"All we, like sheep have gone astray; we have turned everyone to his own way, and the Lord hath laid on him the iniquity of us all" (Isaiah 53:6).

"Sure as you're born, you are gonna die." The King (Elvis) once put it this way; it's now or never. Perhaps.

May God bless you.

About the Author

Tom Hoskins grew up in Davis and Winters, California, near Lake Berryessa. After attending San Jose State and Stanford Universities, he taught science and physical education near the Bay Area for thirty years. Having taught mostly junior high school and some high school as well, he wrote a book called *When I Was a Kid*, which strove to involve his readers in mentoring our youth, as well as adults. This work is intended to encourage believers as well as awaken nonbelievers to the love of our Lord and Savior. Emphasis is placed on the unavoidable fact that our lives on earth will end and sometimes without notice beforehand. The reader will make a choice about his or her own eternal life even if no action is taken. No choice results in a choice. God bless you.

CPSIA information can be obtained
at www.ICGtesting.com
Printed in the USA
JSHW021631151222
34838JS00001B/88

9 781649 523662